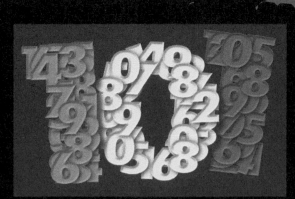 

EMMA LYNCH

CONTENTS

D1630848

SCHOOL'S OUT!

If you could do anything at all next holiday, what would you do? You're going to have weeks and weeks without any *school*! How will you fill the time? You can't just watch telly and play computer games, can you? Admit, it, you're going to get a bit bored. So what else can you do? Why not look outside and see what's on your doorstep?

On your doorstep

The United Kingdom (UK) is one of the Top 10 tourist destinations in the world. It's jam-packed with places to see and things to do. How lucky are we? We live here! What's more, you don't need to travel far or spend a lot of money to enjoy some of the great things that the UK has to offer. You can just step outside ...

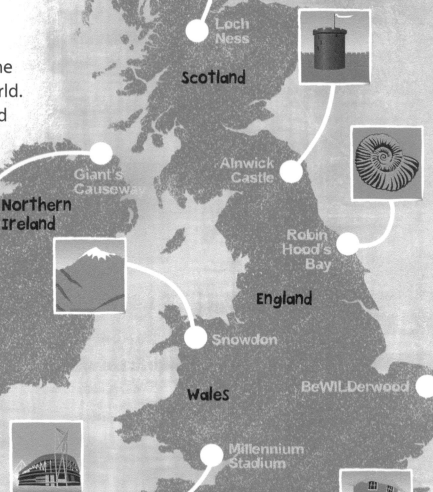

Loch Ness

Scotland

Alnwick Castle

Giant's Causeway

Northern Ireland

Robin Hood's Bay

England

Snowdon

BeWILDerwood

Wales

Millennium Stadium

The UK is made up of England, Scotland, Wales and Northern Ireland. But you knew that already, didn't you?

So what are you waiting for? This book is packed with 101 activities for you to try this holiday. Now, 101 things might sound like a lot. But don't worry – you don't have to do everything. In fact, you don't even need to read this book from start to finish. You can start in the middle!

1 Start a 'To Do' list

Find something in this book that you will *definitely* do in the holidays, and start a list. Some of the activities in this book do not cost any money and you can do them anywhere in the UK. Some activities cost money and you'll need transport, too.

What will *you* do in your next holiday?

August

Mon	Tues	Wed	Thurs	Fri	Sat	Sun
1	2	3	4	5	6	7
8	9	10	11	12	13	14
15	16	17	18	19	20	21
22	23	24	25	26	27	28
29	30	31				

2 VISIT PLANET FOOTBALL

Love it or hate it, football is probably the most popular game in the UK. We have played it and watched it for years. Football fans are passionate about their team and rivalry between teams is the stuff of legends.

Get football fever at the Millennium Stadium

For the ultimate football experience, why not watch a match at the Millennium Stadium in Cardiff? It opened in June 1999 and attracts over a million visitors each year. They come to watch football finals, as well as rugby, motorsports and music events in this impressive venue.

FAST FACT

Legendary Manchester United player, Bobby Charlton, gave Old Trafford the nickname 'The Theatre of Dreams'.

FACT FILE

Millennium Stadium	
UEFA rating	5 stars
Games hosted	FIFA World Cup and **UEFA** European Cup qualifying matches, FA Community Shield, FA and Carling Cup finals, Olympic 2012 football games
Capacity	74 500 spectators
Roof type	**Retractable** roof so different kinds of events can take place all year round
Roof opening time	20 minutes
Number of toilets	760

3 Be wowed by Wembley

Take a tour of Wembley Stadium, London. See the dressing rooms, walk down the players' tunnel, climb up the trophy winners' step and imagine the roar of the crowd as you lift the trophy like your hero.

4 Take a tour

Are you mad about Manchester United FC? Discover the story behind one of the world's greatest teams at the Old Trafford Museum and Tour Centre.

5 Soak up the atmosphere

Ever heard of the Kop? Enjoy a game from the world-famous stand at Liverpool FC's Anfield Stadium.

6 Keep it local

They might not be in the Premiership yet, but with the support of fans like you, who knows how far your local team could go?

7 Get involved

Join a local youth football team. Make new friends and improve your footie skills.

8 Have a kick-about

Which of your heroes will you be today? Use jumpers for goalposts and have a kick-about with friends.

Ever imagined what it would be like to be royalty? How do you fancy strutting around a castle and bossing everyone around?

King of the castle

The UK has a huge number of castles, built throughout its long history. Some are in ruins but others have been well preserved or rebuilt and they are open to the public. Imagine what life was like there hundreds of years ago ...

Sign up for Knight School

Beautiful Alnwick Castle is in Northumberland. It was built almost 1000 years ago. It is open to the public, so you can take a tour of the castle, watch birds of prey demonstrations and even try your hand at archery! If you can't get to Northumberland, you can also see Alnwick in the Harry Potter films – it is featured as Hogwarts School of Witchcraft and Wizardry!

FAST FACT
Alnwick is the second largest lived-in castle in England.

10 Listen for gunshot

Listen to the 1 o'clock gun at Edinburgh Castle, Scotland. This is fired at 1 o'clock, six days a week and has been since 1861, when it was used as a time signal for nearby ships.

11 Have a banquet

Step back into medieval times in the banqueting hall of Carrickfergus Castle, Northern Ireland.

12 Go local

Visit a historic building near where you live, like a stately home, the town hall, a museum or an old mill.

CALLING ALL HEROES!

Do you have the courage and determination to become a knight?

Find out at Alnwick Castle.

Dress as a knight and learn sword-fighting and jousting skills.

Pass your challenges to be awarded the title of Knight.

BE WARNED: ONLY THE NOBLEST KNIGHTS WILL SUCCEED.

DRAGON QUEST

Knights needed to save the castle from ferocious dragons!

Learn from the Dragon Master.

Dare you enter the dragon's lair?

Prepare to face ghosts, monsters and a hall of mirrors before you meet the dragon.

ONLY THE BRAVE NEED APPLY ...

"I liked the sword-fighting best."
Callum, aged 8

"My brother was scared, but I wasn't. The dragon quest was cool."
Annie, aged 9

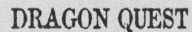

13 Go jousting

Grab a broom, put a saucepan on your head and have a jousting tournament. (Please don't hurt each other or get the pan stuck!)

14 Draw your own

Design and draw the castle you'd like to live in. Don't forget towers, a moat and **crenellations**.

Want to own your own castle? Go to idea 44 to find out how you can.

15 WEIRD WINS

Did you know that the UK is home to some of the weirdest and wackiest competitions in the world? From bog-snorkelling in Powys, Wales to worm-charming in Cheshire, there's something for everyone ... even the worms!

Conquer the conker

Visit the World Conker Championships in Oundle, Northamptonshire. The winner is crowned with conkers on the Conker Throne.

You can start a game of conkers by saying "Obli obli oh, my first go".

How to play conkers

1. Collect conkers.
2. Choose a big conker. Ask an adult to bore a hole in it.
3. Push a piece of string through it and tie a knot at one end.
4. The string needs to wrap around your hand and hang down about 25 cm.
5. Face your **opponent**, holding your conker still.
6. Your opponent swings their conker at yours. If they hit it, then it's your turn. If they miss, they get two more turns.
7. If the strings tangle, then shout 'Snag!' first to get an extra shot.
8. Take turns to strike until one conker is destroyed.
9. The winning conker can battle on!

CONKER CHAMPIONSHIP RULES

Do not make conkers harder! This means you can not:

- soak your conker in vinegar
- bake it for half an hour
- store it in the dark for a year!

16 Get cheesy

Watch a cheesy chase at the cheese rolling competition at Cooper's Hill in Gloucestershire.

17 Go gurning

Visit the World Gurning Championships at Egremont Crab Fair, Cumbria and see people pull the most bizarre faces possible.

18 Watch a caber toss

See men in kilts tossing the **caber** at the Cowal Highland Gathering, Dunoon, Scotland.

19 Get on a roll

Go orange racing in Totnes, Devon. Winners have to prove that the orange they finish with is the one they started with!

20 Be the best

Hold your own conker championship. Will you become the ultimate conker champion?

21 Gross your friends out

Hold your own gurning competition. Take photos and give awards.

FAST FACT

If a conker has won two battles, it is a two-er. If it wins another it becomes a three-er, and so on.

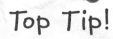

Top Tip!
For a great gurn, it helps if you have no teeth!

22 MONSTER HUNT

Ever seen a very big cat? No, I mean *really* big ... All around the UK there are reports of mysterious beasts that are too big to be pets living out in the wild. Why not turn monster hunter and track down one for yourself?

Hunt for Nessie

The most famous 'monster' in the UK is the Loch Ness Monster. One theory is that the Loch Ness Monster is a plesiosaur living in the loch. A plesiosaur is a sea-living reptile from the time of the dinosaurs. Could a plesiosaur have survived in the deep, dark lake all these years?

FACT FILE

LOCH NESS	
Location	Scotland
Meaning	'Loch' means lake
Length	36.2 km long
Width	1.7 km wide
Depth	227 metres
Amount of water	more than all the lakes of England and Wales put together

MONSTER HUNTER

STEP ON BOARD THE 'MONSTER HUNTER' FOR A MONSTER OF A TRIP!

Take a one-hour trip around Loch Ness.

See where Nessie has been spotted before.

Listen to the sounds below the water.

If Nessie is out there, we will find her - and you could be part of the excitement too. You never know when Nessie will next appear!

Don't miss out on the chance to spot the world's most mysterious lake monster!

1 HOUR TRIP ONLY £5 PER PERSON

MONSTROUS AUTUMN SAVINGS! BUY ONE FULL-PRICE TICKET AND GET A CHILD'S TICKET FREE!

23 Track down a beast

A big, panther-like cat has been spotted many times over the years on Bodmin Moor, in Cornwall. It has been nicknamed 'The Beast of Bodmin'.

24 Turn dino hunter

Track down 'monsters' from the past at The Dinosaur Museum in Dorchester.

25 Keep your eyes peeled

Look out for unusual animal tracks and listen out for howling noises at night ...

FAST FACT

There have been many photographs of 'Nessie'. The most famous one is called 'The Surgeon's Photograph' and was taken in 1934. It was later proved to be a hoax.

FAST FACT

Stories of a water monster living near the loch go back as far as the 6th century!

Want to find creatures that lived many years ago? Go to idea 38 to find out how.

Local parks, recreation grounds, district parks, country parks, national parks ... Did you know there were so many green spaces in the UK?

Find some space

From local parks where you can kick a ball around right up to beautiful national parks and exciting theme parks, the UK is chock-full of green spaces to enjoy.

Go wild at BeWILDerwood

Have you ever seen a Boggle? Been chased by a Twiggle or bamboozled by a Crocklebog? No? You've never been bewildered by BeWILDerwood then. This park in Norfolk promises outdoor adventure in 50 acres of forest, along with a cast of strange forest characters.

In BeWILDerwood, you can:
- climb in and out of treehouses
- ride along zipwires
- cross jungle bridges
- build your own den
- travel down giant slides
- visit a village in the trees
- go on a boat ride across the scary lake
- run along a rickety bridge between the treetops.

What does 'Nemesis' mean?

27 ## Meet your 'Nemesis'

Enjoy a thrilling ride at a theme park. Are you brave enough to ride the 'Nemesis' at Alton Towers in Staffordshire?

28 ## Climb every mountain

Walk along the Brecon Horseshoe, in the Brecon Beacons National Park.

29 ## Get on your bike

Enjoy a safe ride on the cycle paths of Alyn Waters Country Park, Wrexham. There are loads of cycle paths all over the UK. Why don't you find out about the ones near you?

30 ## Get some fresh air

Visit a local park where you live. Take a football and pack a picnic.

Be careful around Mildred, the thorny Crocklebog. She sneezes water from her nose!

NIGHT AT THE MUSEUM

Would you believe the UK has a whopping 2500 museums?! There are museums all about people, science, nature, war, transport, childhood, film ... the list goes on. You're sure to find one you enjoy and many are free to visit. So go on, spend a night (or day!) at the museum ...

Try rocket science

Do you ever wonder how machines work? Or how our bodies work? The Science Museum in London can answer all your questions. This vast museum is packed full of amazing things to see, hear, watch and do.

- See inventions that have changed our world in the Making the Modern World Gallery. You can see the first calculator and the Apollo 10 command module.

- Find out all about yourself in the Who Am I? Gallery. You can even **morph** your face to see how you'll look when you're old!

- Some of the earliest planes are in the Flight Gallery. Why not have a go in a flight simulator just like the ones used to train pilots?

The Making the Modern World Gallery at The Science Museum. The Museum attracts 2.5 million visitors a year!

BERTI, a life-sized human robot can play scissors, paper, stone with you.

Come face to face with real dinosaurs! See idea 24.

32 Don't get big-headed
You can see real shrunken heads at the Pitt Rivers Museum in Oxford – gross and fascinating!

33 Be a TV star
At the National Media Museum in Bradford you can see how TV shows and films are made, and star in your own TV show.

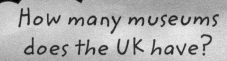
How many museums does the UK have?

34 Don't touch!
Look at over 10 000 toys and models from the last 100 years at The Brighton Toy and Model Museum.

35 Get stuck in
At Eureka, in Halifax you can try out hundreds of hands-on exhibits. This National Children's Museum lets you explore and find out about the world around you!

36 'Mower' interesting!
Why not visit the British Lawnmower Museum in Southport?

37 On your doorstep
Visit a local museum and become a history detective!

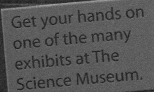
Get your hands on one of the many exhibits at The Science Museum.

FACT FILE

Strange UK museums
Do you know of a stranger museum than these ones?
- Dog Collar Museum, Kent
- Mustard Museum, Norwich
- Pencil Museum, Keswick

The UK has got more coastline than you can shake a stick at! The landscape changes as you travel around the UK, from wild, craggy cliffs and crashing waves to still rock pools, calm seas, and sandy beaches.

Go Jurassic

Hunt down a Jurassic fossil in Robin Hood's Bay in Yorkshire. The best time to find fossils is after a winter storm, when the rocks have come loose from the cliffs.

How to find a fossil

1. Look for **sedimentary** rocks made up of layers of mud, sand and seashells.
2. Collect rocks that have just been swept in by the sea.
3. Collect rocks that have freshly fallen from the cliffs above.
4. Ask the adult to break the rocks apart with the chisel pick.
5. Check for fossils inside.
6. Keep a record of your finds.

You will need:

- sturdy boots
- a chisel pick
- a notebook and pen
- a big bag
- an adult to help you.

This ammonite fossil is 180 million years old.

FAST FACT
The ammonite was a mollusc, a bit like a giant snail.

39 Ride a wave
Try windsurfing at Portrush Whiterocks Beach, Northern Ireland.

40 Get funky
Listen to music on Brighton Beach.

41 See the lights
See Blackpool's Illuminations light up the sky.

42 Feeling crabby?
Go crabbing in Pembrokeshire. (Remember to put the crabs back afterwards ...)

43 Get sand in your toes
Run down the sand dunes in Northumberland.

44 Grab a bucket and spade
Time to build your own castle ... out of sand, on the beach in South Devon. Get some design ideas from idea 14.

45 Look out to sea
Skim stones and count fishing boats in Dorset.

46 Stroll along the pier
Many UK seaside towns have piers which you can walk along. Have a go on the arcades, or just enjoy the view.

47 HAVE A SWEET TREAT

Now here's a good excuse to eat sweets! Different parts of the UK are famous for their sweets and cakes. Why not give your taste buds a treat and try some of the delicious sweets you can find around the UK.

Enjoy a scrumptious day at Cadbury World

Have you ever wanted to visit Willy Wonka's chocolate factory? Would you like to go to a place with chocolate everywhere, all around you, so you can smell it, touch it, taste it, roll around in it?!

You can do all of these things at Cadbury World, Birmingham (well, maybe not roll around in it – you'd probably get thrown out). You can ride a chocolate Beanmobile, see chocolate being made, see yourself made out of chocolate and even make your own chocolate experiments and treats.

FACT FILE

Cadbury World	
Location	Bournville, near Birmingham
Date opened	14th August 1990
Cost to build	£6 million approximately
Visitors per year	Over 500 000

Watch the experts make chocolate at Cadbury World.

Top Tip!
Remember to brush your teeth afterwards!

 48 Make your own
All you need is one grown-up and a recipe for fudge and you're good to go.

 49 Chew a stick
Suck some Blackpool rock to remember your holiday. It can take up to 10 years of practice for Blackpool rock makers to get the rock lettering technique perfect!

 50 Have a cuppa
Have a Cornish cream tea. Do you put the jam or the cream on first?

 51 Pack rations
Pack Kendal mint cake to give you energy on a long walk. This sugar-packed treat comes from Kendal in Cumbria.

 52 Lick some liquorice
Try a liquorice Pomfret cake at the liquorice festival, Pontefract.

 53 Try a taste of honey
Munch a piece of honeycomb fresh from a local beekeeper.

 54 Can't get to the coast?
Have an ice-cream and imagine you're there!

The UK's amazing landscapes have been formed by our climate, seas and coastal winds. We have hills, valleys, mountains, cliffs, wild moors, rolling downs, dales, fens, woods and forests, not to mention some incredible natural wonders.

Follow in the footsteps of giants

Visit the Giant's Causeway, County Antrim. This eerie landscape in Northern Ireland is made up of around 40 000 hexagonal columns of **basalt** rock leading into the sea.

A tall tale

Legend says the **causeway** was formed by a giant called Finn MacCool. MacCool wanted to fight his enemy Benandonner so he hurled rocks into the sea to make a path. When Benandonner got across, he found MacCool dressed as a baby. Amazed by the size of the 'baby', he thought about how big his father must be, and ran back to Scotland, destroying most of the causeway.

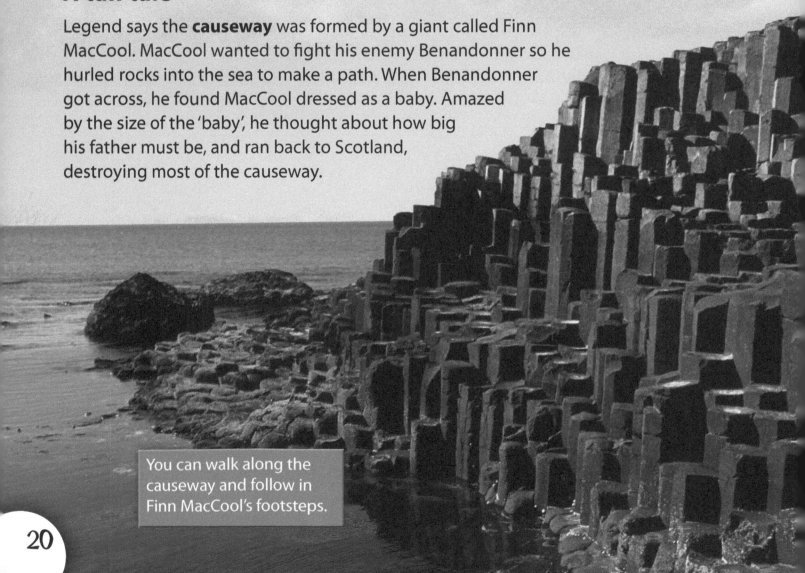

You can walk along the causeway and follow in Finn MacCool's footsteps.

How many columns make up the Giant's Causeway?

How much wider is Loch Lomond than Loch Ness?

56 See the Needles by cable car

The Needles are three enormous stacks of chalk that rise out of the sea off the mainland of the Isle of Wight.

57 Find the key to Durdle Door

Enjoy a picnic on the beach next to the limestone arch in Dorset.

58 Go back to the Ice Age

Cheddar Gorge is the deepest **gorge** in England. The 9000-year-old 'Cheddar Man' was found in one of its many caves.

59 Have a dip

Lulworth Cove in Dorset is the most perfect example of a cove.

60 Go canoeing

Loch Lomond in Scotland is the UK's largest lake, at 39 km long and 8 km wide in places.

61 Climb a pike

Scafell Pike in the Lake District is the highest peak in England. Get climbing!

62 Go on nature watch

Go for a nature walk where you live and look for signs of the changing seasons.

63 Don't stop until the top

Climb a big hill near where you live and find out how high it is.

64 Go bug-hunting

Look under rocks and twigs and see how many different bugs you can find!

FAST FACT
The Giant's Causeway was actually formed by volcanic eruptions 50–60 million years ago.

65 TURN A PAGE

Have you ever wished you could go to school at Hogwarts or find a magical land at the back of your wardrobe? When you read a fantastic story you can see the places, characters and action in your head. Many of the places in books are based on real locations, so you can visit them and enjoy your own adventures there.

Find a golden ticket

Find out all about the creator of Willy Wonka at the Roald Dahl Museum and Story Centre, in Great Missenden, Buckinghamshire. Dahl lived in the village for 36 years and wrote all his children's stories there. You can explore a **replica** of the hut in his garden where Dahl wrote his stories. You can even go on a Village Trail to see some of the places he describes in his books. Or try your hand at chocolate-decorating or puppet-making!

The replica of Dahl's writing hut, inside the Roald Dahl Museum.

FACT FILE

- Roald Dahl was born in Llandaff, Wales on 13th September 1916.
- Before he became a writer, he was a pilot officer in the Royal Air Force.
- He became interested in writing children's books from making up bedtime stories for his daughters.
- Matilda sold half a million paperback books in 6 months.
- Roald couldn't type. He always used a pencil to write.

For more chocolately fun see idea 47.

66 Explore Swallowdale

Climb The Old Man of Coniston in the Lake District and see the 'Swallowdale' of *Swallows and Amazons*.

67 Visit Toad Hall

Follow Mole, Ratty, Badger and Mr Toad's adventures at the *Wind in the Willows* Exhibition at the River and Rowing Museum, Henley on Thames.

68 Bring on the Bard

Travel to Stratford and visit Shakespeare's birthplace.

69 Have a punt

Drift down Oxford's River Isis by punt and see where Lewis Carroll created *Alice in Wonderland*.

70 Get into the closet

Visit Belfast, birthplace of CS Lewis, and see a statue of the author with the wardrobe leading to Narnia.

71 Please look after this bear

See where Paddington Bear got his name at London's Paddington Station.

72 Sprinkle some magic

Visit Platform $9\frac{3}{4}$ at Kings Cross Station and follow in the footsteps of Harry Potter!

73 See it in your head

Can't get to any of these places? Visit your local library and read about them in the books.

Have you read any of Roald Dahl's books? Which one's your favourite?

74 Go Wild

Rabbits and goldfish make great pets, but why not check out some really wild animals? You'd be surprised how many types of animal make their homes here. They may live not too far away from you ...

Meet a very big dog

Hundreds of years ago wolves roamed around Europe and the UK. They were hunted to extinction in the UK around 300 years ago. Now, you can see European grey wolves at the Highlands Wildlife Park, Kincraig in Scotland. A male and a female have been introduced to Wolf Wood and it is hoped that they will breed.

FACT FILE

- Wolves live in packs and the whole pack takes care of the pups.
- Wolves use facial expressions, growls and barks, body language and howling to communicate with each other.
- Wolves eat deer, hares, sheep, birds, mice, reptiles, insects, berries and plants.

FAST FACT
Wolves are the largest member of the dog family.

75 Be a badger watcher
Watch out for badgers living near you. Look for claw marks on tree trunks. Do not disturb the badgers or the **sett**.

76 Hello deer
The red deer is the most famous of Scotland's animals and you can see some in the Highlands.

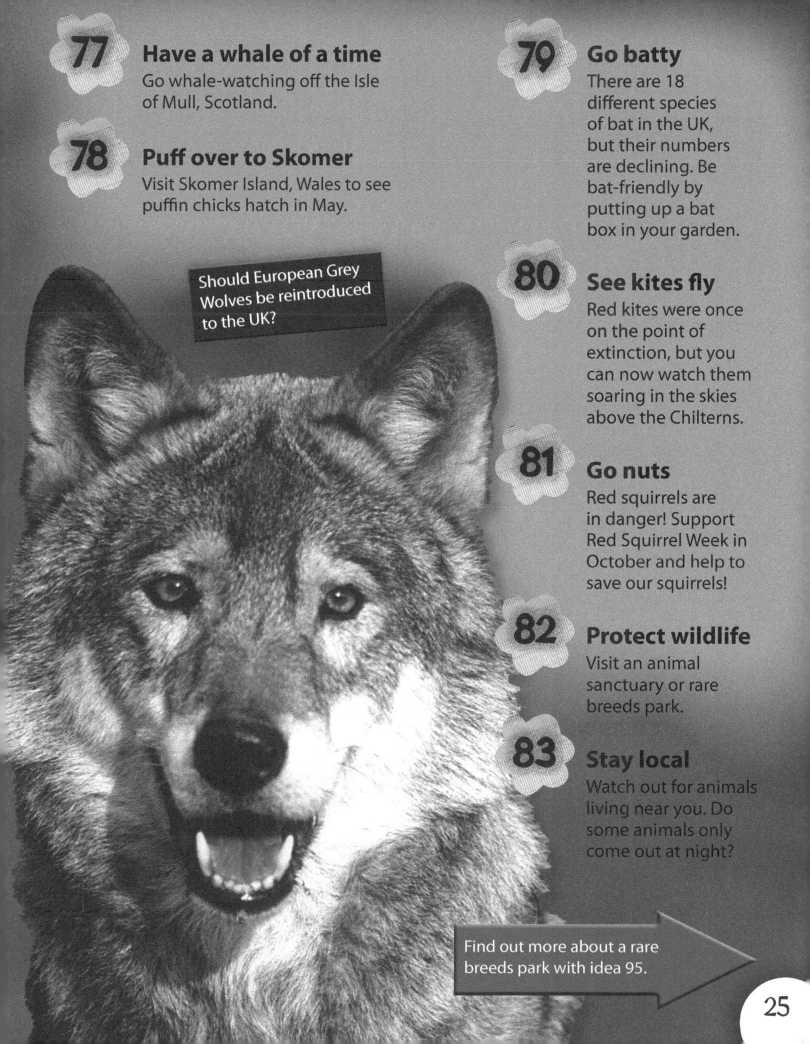

77 Have a whale of a time
Go whale-watching off the Isle of Mull, Scotland.

78 Puff over to Skomer
Visit Skomer Island, Wales to see puffin chicks hatch in May.

Should European Grey Wolves be reintroduced to the UK?

79 Go batty
There are 18 different species of bat in the UK, but their numbers are declining. Be bat-friendly by putting up a bat box in your garden.

80 See kites fly
Red kites were once on the point of extinction, but you can now watch them soaring in the skies above the Chilterns.

81 Go nuts
Red squirrels are in danger! Support Red Squirrel Week in October and help to save our squirrels!

82 Protect wildlife
Visit an animal sanctuary or rare breeds park.

83 Stay local
Watch out for animals living near you. Do some animals only come out at night?

Find out more about a rare breeds park with idea 95.

84 DITCH THE CAR

What's the best way to see the UK? By boat? From the air? A car will take you from A to B, but there are so many more exciting and picturesque ways to get around the UK.

Steam to the summit

Snowdon dominates Snowdonia National Park and you can enjoy spectacular views from the Snowdon Mountain Railway. The railway opened in 1896. Before then the only way to the top of Snowdon was on foot ... or by donkey!

FAST FACT
According to legend, the knights of King Arthur sleep below Mount Snowdon.

Summit Station

The route along the Snowdon Mountain Railway.

LLANBERIS

Llanberis Station

85 Go by tram
By 2016 Manchester will have 60 miles of track, at least 99 stops and the largest tram network in the UK.

86 Don't get wet!
Take Newcastle's underground Metro train all the way to the seaside at Whitley Bay.

Journey to the top

The railway runs through spring, summer and early autumn.

Journey up over viaducts and past waterfalls.

Travel through forest and up increasingly steep tracks to the summit.

Be warned – in high winds the train stops 5/8ths of the way up the mountain!

Watch out for ravens and mountain goats. on the way up.

Ride back down on the train, or walk down on foot.

FAST FACT
Snowdon is 1085 m high and is the highest mountain in Wales.

Which animals might you see on your way up Snowdon?

87 Rise high and drop down
Taking the cable car across the Derwent Valley is only the beginning. Once at the top you can travel underground into the Great Masson Cavern.

88 Get on your bike
Follow the Isle's of Wight's cycle tracks from Cowes to Newport.

89 Fill up with hot air
For a panoramic view, ride in a hot air balloon over the South Downs.

90 Drift away
Drift from Stafford to Worcester on a narrow boat and see England from its canals.

91 Get your skates on
Find your local skateboard park and land a nollie heelflip ...

92 Roll with it
Strap on some rollerblades and go for a spin in the park.

93 Keep on running
Pull on your trainers and go for a run ... or jog ... or walk.

Why not visit one of the 300 000 working farms in the UK? Farmers grow crops (food, like wheat and barley) and raise livestock (animals like sheep and cows) to sell. Some farmers let the public visit their farms.

Get mucky at Meanwood

Meanwood Valley Urban Farm was built near Leeds in 1980. It is a working farm that is also a centre for **community** and environmental work. Here are some of the things you can do:

- Meet the animals. There are goats, donkeys, sheep, cows and hens.

- Find out about animals and the products we get from them.

- Learn about free-range farming and rare breeds.

- See how fruit, vegetables and herbs are grown in a market garden.

- Explore different wildlife habitats like ponds, woodland and meadows.

greenhouse
goat
shrubs
pond
playground
trees
solar panels
allotments
cow field

Where to find everything at Meanwood Valley Urban Farm

FACT FILE

Among the animals at Meanwood Valley Urban Farm are the following:
- Dexter cows. These are easy to keep and can stand difficult conditions, which makes them suitable for an urban farm.
- Southdown sheep. These sheep have really woolly faces and high quality wool. They are very friendly, which makes them easy to care for.

FAST FACT
Meanwood Valley Urban Farm runs a mud workshop for school children to investigate soil! Sounds messy ...

95 Feed the babies
Visit the Cotswold Farm Park near Stow-on-the-Wold and feed the spring lambs.

96 Be a-maized
Find your way around the maize maze at Tulleys Farm in West Sussex.

97 Hop on board
Take a tractor ride around Hall Hill Farm, Durham and see the goats, sheep and alpacas.

98 See a harvest Moon
A harvest Moon is a full Moon close to 22 or 23 September. It rises soon after the Sun sets. Harvest Moons got their name because farmers could continue to bring in their crops even after the Sun had set, without having to wait in darkness for the Moon to rise.

99 Grow your own
Plant cress seeds in damp cotton wool. When the cress grows, you can harvest your own crop.

100 Get fruity on a farm
Go strawberry-picking in June and July. Just remember to put them in the basket and not in your mouth!

FAST FACT
France and Belgium both have museums about the strawberry.

Last but not least ...
Come on, you could have done 101 amazing things this holiday. Surely you should send someone a postcard?!

POST CARD

Hi Tom!

Today I went to the Roald Dahl Museum. I saw an exact replica of his writing hut and walked around the village he lived in.

Wish you were here!

Max

1ST
ROYAL MAIL

Tom Walker

2 Lower Glebe Road

Birmingham

UK

GLOSSARY INDEX

basalt dark rock formed by hardening melted earth

caber long heavy wooden pole tossed end over end as a demonstration of strength in Scottish highland games

causeway pathway that is raised above wet ground or water

community people living in an area

crenellations rampart built around the top of a castle with regular gaps for firing arrows

gorge deep narrow passage with steep rocky sides

morph change in form

opponent someone who takes an opposite position; who opposes another

replica exact copy

retractable something which can be pulled out and pulled back in

sedimentary type of rock that contains rounded grains in layers

sett badger's den

UEFA Union of European Football Associations, which represents most of the national football associations of Europe